The War on Terror

American history, Volume 23

Michael Johnson

Published by Harmony House Publishing, 2024.

While every precaution has been taken in the preparation of this book, the publisher assumes no responsibility for errors or omissions, or for damages resulting from the use of the information contained herein.

THE WAR ON TERROR

First edition. April 4, 2024.

Copyright © 2024 Michael Johnson.

ISBN: 979-8224397716

Written by Michael Johnson.

Table of Contents

To all those who have been impacted by the scourge of terrorism, whether directly or indirectly, this book is dedicated to you. Your resilience, courage, and unwavering spirit in the face of adversity inspire us to continue the fight against global terrorism. May this book serve as a testament to our shared commitment to building a safer, more peaceful world for generations to come.

Chapter 1: The Rise of Terrorism

Introduction:

Terrorism, in its most basic definition, refers to the use of violence or intimidation to achieve political, religious, or ideological goals. It is a tactic employed by individuals, groups, or states to instill fear, create chaos, and achieve their objectives through coercion. While terrorism has been a part of human history for centuries, its modern manifestations have been shaped by a complex interplay of historical, political, social, and technological factors. Understanding the roots and evolution of terrorism is crucial in comprehending the contemporary global landscape of conflict and security.

Historical Context:

To grasp the origins of modern terrorism, we must delve into history to explore the socio-political conditions that gave rise to its emergence. While acts of violence for political ends have occurred throughout history, the late 19th and early 20th centuries witnessed significant developments that laid the groundwork for the modern terrorist movements we see today.

One pivotal event was the Russian Revolution of 1917, which led to the establishment of the Soviet Union under Bolshevik rule. The revolution inspired revolutionary movements worldwide and gave rise to leftist ideologies that advocated for the overthrow of existing governments through violent means. This period saw the emergence of groups like the Bolsheviks, anarchists, and socialist revolutionaries who employed terrorism as a tool to achieve their revolutionary goals.

Another influential factor was the decolonization movements that swept across Asia, Africa, and the Middle East in the aftermath of World War II. As colonized peoples sought to break free from imperial rule, nationalist movements emerged, some of which resorted to terrorism as a means of resistance against colonial powers. Examples include the Algerian National Liberation Front (FLN) fighting against French colonial rule and the Zionist paramilitary groups in British-controlled Palestine.

Key Events:

Several key events throughout the 20th century shaped the trajectory of modern terrorism, laying the foundation for the global phenomenon we see today. These events served as catalysts for the evolution of terrorist tactics, ideologies, and organizational structures.

One such event was the assassination of Archduke Franz Ferdinand of Austria-Hungary in 1914 by a Bosnian Serb nationalist, Gavrilo Princip. This act precipitated the outbreak of World War I and highlighted the potential of terrorism to spark broader conflicts and destabilize entire regions. The use of political assassination as a tool of terrorism became increasingly prevalent in the years that followed.

The interwar period saw the rise of fascist and totalitarian regimes in Europe, notably Nazi Germany and Mussolini's Italy, which employed state-sponsored terrorism to suppress dissent and persecute minority groups. The brutal tactics of these regimes, including the systematic targeting of Jews, political opponents, and civilians, demonstrated the capacity for organized violence on an unprecedented scale.

The aftermath of World War II witnessed the birth of the state of Israel in 1948 and the ensuing Arab-Israeli conflict. This protracted conflict gave rise to Palestinian militant groups such as the Palestine Liberation Organization (PLO) and Hamas, which employed terrorism as a means of resistance against Israeli occupation. The Arab-Israeli conflict remains a central flashpoint in the geopolitics of the Middle East and continues to fuel acts of terrorism to this day.

Another watershed moment was the Iranian Revolution of 1979, which overthrew the Western-backed monarchy of Shah Mohammad Reza Pahlavi and established an Islamic republic under the leadership of Ayatollah Khomeini. The revolution inspired Islamist movements worldwide and fueled the spread of radical ideologies, culminating in the emergence of groups like Hezbollah, Hamas, and later, Al-Qaeda.

The 1970s and 1980s also witnessed a wave of international terrorism, marked by high-profile attacks such as the hostage-taking at the 1972 Munich Olympics by the Palestinian group Black September, and the bombing of the U.S. Marine barracks in Beirut in 1983 by Hezbollah. These events underscored the transnational nature of terrorism and its ability to transcend borders and jurisdictions.

Conclusion:

The rise of terrorism is a complex and multifaceted phenomenon shaped by historical, political, and socio-economic factors. From the Russian Revolution to the Arab-Israeli conflict, key events throughout the 20th century have influenced the evolution of terrorist movements and tactics. Understanding this historical context is essential in formulating effective strategies to address the contemporary challenges posed by terrorism in the 21st century. As we shall explore in subsequent chapters, the roots of modern terrorism run deep, and addressing its underlying causes requires a comprehensive and multifaceted approach.

Chapter 2: 9/11: The Turning Point

On the morning of September 11, 2001, the world watched in horror as a series of coordinated terrorist attacks unfolded in the United States, forever altering the course of history and reshaping global geopolitics. The events of that fateful day would come to be known simply as 9/11, a turning point that ushered in a new era of fear, uncertainty, and unprecedented challenges for the United States and the world at large.

Detailed Account of the September 11, 2001, Terrorist Attacks:

The meticulously planned and executed attacks on 9/11 targeted symbols of American power and prestige, striking at the heart of the nation's economic and military might. At 8:46 a.m. Eastern Time, American Airlines Flight 11, hijacked by five Al-Qaeda terrorists, crashed into the North Tower of the World Trade Center in New York City, instantly killing hundreds of people and trapping thousands more inside the burning skyscraper.

As the world watched in shock and disbelief, 17 minutes later, at 9:03 a.m., United Airlines Flight 175, also hijacked by Al-Qaeda operatives, slammed into the South Tower of the World Trade Center, exacerbating the chaos and devastation. The twin towers, iconic symbols of America's economic prowess and global influence, collapsed within hours, leaving a gaping void in the New York City skyline and claiming the lives of nearly 3,000 innocent victims.

Simultaneously, at 9:37 a.m., American Airlines Flight 77 crashed into the Pentagon, the headquarters of the United States Department of Defense, in Arlington, Virginia. The attack resulted in extensive damage to the Pentagon's western side and claimed the lives of 125 military personnel and civilians inside the building.

Amidst the chaos and confusion, a fourth hijacked airliner, United Airlines Flight 93, bound for Washington, D.C., was heroically brought down by passengers who thwarted the hijackers' plans, sacrificing their lives to prevent further destruction. The plane crashed into a field in Shanksville, Pennsylvania, at 10:03 a.m., averting another potential catastrophe and inspiring a nation with acts of bravery and selflessness in the face of unimaginable terror.

Immediate Aftermath and Shockwaves Felt Around the World:

In the aftermath of the 9/11 attacks, the United States and the world grappled with the enormity of the tragedy and its far-reaching implications. The shockwaves reverberated across continents, triggering a wave of fear, anger, and solidarity as nations rallied to express their condolences and offer support to the grieving American people.

Within the United States, the immediate aftermath of 9/11 was characterized by a sense of collective shock and mourning, as the nation came to terms with the staggering loss of life and the sheer scale of the devastation. Images of the collapsing towers, the billowing smoke, and the frantic rescue efforts dominated television screens and newspaper headlines, searing themselves into the collective consciousness of a traumatized nation.

In the days and weeks following the attacks, the United States mobilized its resources and launched a massive rescue and recovery operation, with thousands of first responders, volunteers, and emergency personnel working tirelessly around the clock to search for survivors and clear the rubble. The outpouring of support and solidarity from ordinary citizens and communities across the country served as a testament to the resilience and strength of the American spirit in the face of adversity.

Internationally, the shockwaves of 9/11 reverberated far and wide, eliciting expressions of solidarity and condemnation from governments and leaders around the world. From Europe to Asia, from Africa to Latin America, nations stood in solidarity with the United States, offering condolences, condemning the senseless violence, and pledging support in the global fight against terrorism.

Analysis of the Impact of 9/11 on American Foreign Policy and National Security:

The 9/11 attacks had far-reaching implications for American foreign policy and national security, ushering in a new era of heightened vigilance, military interventionism, and securitization. In the immediate aftermath of the attacks, President George W. Bush declared a "War on Terror" and vowed to hunt down and punish those responsible for the heinous acts of terrorism.

The Bush administration swiftly identified the terrorist organization Al-Qaeda and its leader, Osama bin Laden, as the masterminds behind the 9/11 attacks, laying the groundwork for a global campaign to dismantle the terrorist network and its affiliates. The invasion of Afghanistan in October 2001 marked the beginning of the U.S.-led military intervention in the region, aimed at ousting the Taliban regime and disrupting Al-Qaeda's operational capabilities.

Furthermore, the Bush administration pursued a doctrine of preemptive war and regime change, as evidenced by the invasion of Iraq in March 2003, under the pretext of eliminating weapons of mass destruction and removing the tyrannical regime of Saddam Hussein. The decision to invade Iraq and the subsequent occupation of the country would prove to be highly controversial and divisive, sparking intense debate and criticism both domestically and internationally.

The 9/11 attacks also precipitated a paradigm shift in American foreign policy, as the United States adopted a more assertive and unilateral approach to combating terrorism and promoting its national interests abroad. The Bush administration's embrace of preventive war, regime change, and unilateralism marked a departure from traditional norms of international diplomacy and multilateral cooperation, straining relations with key allies and undermining America's credibility and moral authority on the world stage.

Moreover, the 9/11 attacks prompted a fundamental reevaluation of America's approach to national security, leading to the enactment of sweeping counterterrorism measures and the expansion of executive powers in the name of protecting the homeland. The passage of the USA PATRIOT Act, the establishment of the Department of Homeland Security, and the implementation of enhanced surveillance and intelligence-gathering capabilities represented significant shifts in U.S. policy and law enforcement practices, raising concerns about civil liberties, privacy rights, and the erosion of democratic norms.

In conclusion, the events of September 11, 2001, marked a seismic shift in the trajectory of American foreign policy and national security, ushering in an era of unprecedented challenges and complexities in the fight against terrorism.

The attacks served as a wake-up call to the vulnerabilities of the modern world and the urgent need for collective action and cooperation to address the evolving threats of terrorism and violent extremism. As we shall explore in subsequent chapters, the legacy of 9/11 continues to shape the contours of global conflict and security in the 21st century, underscoring the enduring importance of vigilance, resilience, and solidarity in confronting the scourge of terrorism.

Chapter 3: The Bush Doctrine

Exploration of President George W. Bush's Response to 9/11:

In the wake of the devastating terrorist attacks of September 11, 2001, President George W. Bush faced the monumental task of crafting a comprehensive response that would not only address the immediate threat posed by terrorist organizations like Al-Qaeda but also reshape America's approach to national security and foreign policy in the post-9/11 world. With the nation reeling from the deadliest terrorist attack in its history and the specter of further attacks looming large, President Bush sought to rally the American people and mobilize the full resources of the United States in a global campaign against terrorism.

In a televised address to the nation on the evening of September 11, President Bush vowed to hunt down and punish those responsible for the attacks, declaring, "We will make no distinction between the terrorists who committed these acts and those who harbor them." This statement set the tone for the Bush administration's response to 9/11, signaling a departure from the passive containment strategies of the past and a shift towards a more proactive and assertive approach to combating terrorism.

In the days and weeks following the attacks, President Bush marshaled international support for a coordinated military campaign against Al-Qaeda and its Taliban hosts in Afghanistan, culminating in the launch of Operation Enduring Freedom in October 2001. The invasion of Afghanistan aimed to dismantle Al-Qaeda's operational infrastructure, remove the Taliban regime from power, and deny terrorist groups a safe haven from which to plan and launch future attacks against the United States and its allies.

Unveiling the Bush Doctrine and Its Implications for Combating Terrorism:

Central to President Bush's response to 9/11 was the articulation of a new strategic doctrine that would guide America's actions in the global war on terror. This doctrine, commonly referred to as the Bush Doctrine, represented a radical departure from the principles of containment and deterrence that had characterized U.S. foreign policy during the Cold War era. At its core, the Bush Doctrine espoused a doctrine of preemptive self-defense, asserting America's right to take military action against perceived threats before they materialized.

In a speech delivered at the U.S. Military Academy at West Point on June 1, 2002, President Bush outlined the key tenets of the Bush Doctrine, stating, "The United States will use all necessary means to defeat emerging threats before they are fully formed." This doctrine represented a bold assertion of America's prerogative to act unilaterally and preemptively to protect its national security interests, even in the absence of imminent danger or direct provocation.

The Bush Doctrine also emphasized the importance of promoting democracy and freedom as antidotes to terrorism and tyranny. President Bush argued that by spreading the values of liberty and democracy, the United States could undermine the ideological appeal of extremist movements and foster conditions conducive to peace and stability in regions plagued by oppression and conflict. This ideological component of the Bush Doctrine would shape America's approach to nation-building and democratization efforts in the Middle East and beyond, as evidenced by the administration's efforts to promote political reform in countries like Iraq and Afghanistan.

Justification for Preemptive Military Action and Interventionist Policies:

One of the most controversial aspects of the Bush Doctrine was its justification for preemptive military action and interventionist policies aimed at preempting emerging threats and promoting regime change in states perceived to pose a threat to U.S. national security. In the aftermath of 9/11, the Bush administration argued that traditional concepts of deterrence and containment were inadequate in the face of the new and evolving threats posed by transnational terrorist networks and rogue states seeking weapons of mass destruction.

The Bush administration's decision to invade Iraq in March 2003 under the pretext of eliminating weapons of mass destruction and removing the tyrannical regime of Saddam Hussein exemplified the application of the preemptive war doctrine outlined in the Bush Doctrine. Despite lacking conclusive evidence of Iraq's possession of weapons of mass destruction, the administration justified the invasion as a necessary preemptive measure to prevent the proliferation of weapons of mass destruction to terrorist groups and rogue states.

Critics of the Bush Doctrine argued that preemptive war and regime change represented a dangerous departure from established principles of international law and norms of state sovereignty, undermining the credibility of U.S. leadership and exacerbating tensions with key allies and partners. Moreover, the failure to uncover evidence of weapons of mass destruction in Iraq and the protracted and costly military occupation that followed raised serious questions about the wisdom and efficacy of the administration's interventionist policies.

In conclusion, the Bush Doctrine represented a bold and ambitious attempt to redefine America's role in the world in the aftermath of 9/11, advocating for a more assertive and proactive approach to combating terrorism and promoting democracy. While the doctrine articulated a compelling vision of American leadership and moral clarity, its implementation was fraught with challenges and controversies, highlighting the complex trade-offs and unintended consequences of interventionist policies and preemptive military action. As we shall explore in subsequent chapters, the legacy of the Bush Doctrine continues to shape America's foreign policy and national security strategy in the 21st century, underscoring the enduring tensions between the imperatives of security and the constraints of international law and diplomacy.

Chapter 4: Afghanistan: The First Front

Examination of the U.S. Invasion of Afghanistan in Response to 9/11:

The U.S. invasion of Afghanistan in the aftermath of the September 11, 2001, terrorist attacks marked the opening salvo in America's global war on terror. With the Taliban regime providing safe haven to Al-Qaeda and its leader Osama bin Laden, who masterminded the 9/11 attacks, Afghanistan became the primary focus of U.S. military intervention aimed at dismantling terrorist networks and denying them sanctuary.

Operation Enduring Freedom, launched in October 2001, sought to achieve several objectives: ousting the Taliban from power, disrupting Al-Qaeda's operational capabilities, and establishing a stable and democratic government in Afghanistan. The invasion was conducted in collaboration with Afghan opposition forces, including the Northern Alliance, and enjoyed broad international support from NATO allies and other coalition partners.

The U.S.-led coalition employed a combination of air power, special operations forces, and indigenous allies to quickly overthrow the Taliban regime and dismantle Al-Qaeda's infrastructure. Within weeks, major cities and strategic strongholds fell to coalition forces, and the Taliban government was ousted from power. However, the swift military victory would soon give way to a protracted and complex insurgency, as remnants of the Taliban and Al-Qaeda regrouped and launched a guerrilla campaign against coalition forces and the newly established Afghan government.

Role of the Taliban and Al-Qaeda in Afghanistan:

The Taliban, a fundamentalist Islamist movement that emerged in Afghanistan in the early 1990s, seized control of the country in 1996 after years of civil war and chaos. Under the Taliban's draconian rule, Afghanistan became a haven for terrorist groups, including Al-Qaeda, which enjoyed the regime's protection and support in exchange for loyalty and assistance in enforcing Taliban rule.

Al-Qaeda, founded by Osama bin Laden in the late 1980s, established its headquarters in Afghanistan in the 1990s, leveraging the Taliban's hospitality to plan and launch terrorist attacks against the United States and its allies. The 9/11 attacks, orchestrated by Al-Qaeda operatives trained and funded in Afghanistan, catapulted the organization to global infamy and precipitated the U.S.-led invasion that would ultimately dislodge the Taliban regime and dismantle Al-Qaeda's operational network.

Challenges Faced by the U.S. Military in the Afghan Conflict:

While the initial phase of the U.S. military intervention in Afghanistan was characterized by swift and decisive victories, the subsequent stabilization and reconstruction efforts faced numerous challenges and setbacks. The U.S.-led coalition quickly found itself embroiled in a protracted insurgency fueled by a potent mix of tribal rivalries, ethnic tensions, and extremist ideologies, compounded by decades of conflict, poverty, and underdevelopment.

One of the primary challenges faced by coalition forces was the resilience and adaptability of the Taliban insurgency, which regrouped and launched a sustained guerrilla campaign against U.S. and NATO troops and the Afghan government. The Taliban's use of asymmetric warfare tactics, including suicide bombings, improvised explosive devices (IEDs), and hit-and-run attacks, posed a significant threat to coalition forces and undermined efforts to establish security and stability in the country.

Moreover, the U.S. military's focus on counterterrorism operations and hunting down high-value targets like Osama bin Laden and senior Al-Qaeda leaders diverted resources and attention away from broader counterinsurgency and nation-building efforts. The absence of a coherent and coordinated strategy for stabilizing Afghanistan and addressing the root causes of instability and violence allowed the Taliban to exploit grievances and weaknesses in governance, perpetuating a cycle of conflict and insecurity.

Additionally, the challenge of building and sustaining effective Afghan security forces proved to be a daunting task for the U.S.-led coalition. Despite significant investments in training, equipping, and advising Afghan army and police units, endemic corruption, ethnic divisions, and desertion rates undermined the effectiveness and cohesion of Afghan security forces, hindering their ability to assume responsibility for securing the country and combating the insurgency independently.

Furthermore, the complex and volatile regional dynamics surrounding Afghanistan, including the involvement of neighboring countries like Pakistan, Iran, and Russia, added another layer of complexity to the conflict. Pakistan's support for the Taliban and other insurgent groups, in particular, fueled suspicions and tensions between Islamabad and Washington, complicating efforts to achieve a durable political settlement and regional stability.

In conclusion, the U.S. invasion of Afghanistan in response to 9/11 achieved initial military success in overthrowing the Taliban regime and dismantling Al-Qaeda's operational network. However, the subsequent insurgency and nation-building efforts faced numerous challenges and setbacks, including the resilience of the Taliban insurgency, the weaknesses of Afghan security forces, and the complexities of regional politics. As we shall explore in subsequent chapters, the Afghan conflict would evolve into America's longest war, testing the limits of U.S. military power and strategic patience in the pursuit of elusive peace and stability in a war-torn land.

Chapter 5: Iraq: The Controversial Intervention

Analysis of the Decision to Invade Iraq in 2003:

The decision to invade Iraq in 2003 represents one of the most controversial and consequential foreign policy choices in modern American history. Spearheaded by the administration of President George W. Bush, the invasion of Iraq was justified on the grounds of eliminating weapons of mass destruction (WMDs), removing Saddam Hussein from power, and promoting democracy and stability in the Middle East. However, the decision to launch a preemptive war against Iraq was met with skepticism and opposition both domestically and internationally, and its repercussions continue to reverberate to this day.

In the aftermath of the September 11, 2001, terrorist attacks, the Bush administration sought to capitalize on the national mood of fear and vulnerability to advance its broader foreign policy objectives, including the ousting of Saddam Hussein's regime in Iraq. Despite lacking direct evidence linking Iraq to the 9/11 attacks, the administration sought to conflate the threat posed by Al-Qaeda with the purported threat posed by Saddam Hussein's regime, framing Iraq as part of an axis of evil harboring weapons of mass destruction and supporting terrorism.

Moreover, the Bush administration argued that Saddam Hussein's defiance of international disarmament mandates and his alleged pursuit of weapons of mass destruction posed an imminent threat to regional stability and global security, necessitating preemptive military action to remove him from power and eliminate the perceived threat. The administration also cited Iraq's human rights abuses, support for terrorism, and record of aggression against its neighbors as additional justifications for intervention.

Despite widespread skepticism and opposition from key allies and international institutions, including the United Nations Security Council, the Bush administration pressed ahead with its plans for war, bypassing diplomatic efforts to resolve the crisis peacefully and launching a unilateral military invasion of Iraq in March 2003. The decision to invade Iraq would prove to be highly controversial and divisive, fueling intense debate and criticism both domestically and internationally and undermining America's credibility and moral authority on the world stage.

Justifications Presented by the Bush Administration:

The Bush administration presented several justifications for the invasion of Iraq, ranging from national security concerns to humanitarian imperatives to the promotion of democracy and freedom in the Middle East. One of the primary justifications cited by the administration was the alleged threat posed by Iraq's weapons of mass destruction (WMD) programs, including its purported stockpiles of chemical and biological weapons and its pursuit of nuclear weapons capabilities.

The administration argued that Saddam Hussein's regime had repeatedly flouted international disarmament mandates and obstructed efforts by weapons inspectors to verify the extent of its WMD programs, thereby creating a situation of uncertainty and ambiguity that justified preemptive military action to eliminate the perceived threat. Despite the absence of conclusive evidence linking Iraq to the 9/11 attacks or confirming the existence of WMDs, the administration invoked the specter of WMD proliferation and the potential for their use by terrorist groups as a casus belli for war.

Moreover, the Bush administration framed the invasion of Iraq as part of a broader strategy to promote democracy and freedom in the Middle East and advance America's national security interests in the region. By removing Saddam Hussein from power and facilitating the establishment of a democratic and stable government in Iraq, the administration argued that the United States could transform the political landscape of the Middle East, weaken terrorist networks, and enhance regional security and stability.

Furthermore, the administration sought to link the invasion of Iraq to the broader global war on terror, portraying Saddam Hussein's regime as a state sponsor of terrorism and an ally of Al-Qaeda. While there was limited evidence to support direct collaboration between Iraq and Al-Qaeda, the administration sought to exploit public fears and perceptions of terrorism in the aftermath of 9/11 to garner support for its interventionist policies and preemptive war doctrine.

Consequences of the Iraq War on Regional Stability

and Global Perceptions of U.S. Foreign Policy:

The Iraq War had far-reaching consequences for regional stability and global perceptions of U.S. foreign policy, reshaping the geopolitical landscape of the Middle East and fueling anti-American sentiment and insurgency in Iraq and beyond. The toppling of Saddam Hussein's regime and the subsequent power vacuum unleashed a wave of sectarian violence, insurgency, and civil conflict that plunged Iraq into chaos and instability, exacerbating existing tensions and grievances between Sunni and Shia communities and ethnic factions.

Moreover, the U.S.-led occupation and nation-building efforts in Iraq were marked by widespread human rights abuses, including torture, extrajudicial killings, and the erosion of civil liberties, further alienating the Iraqi population and undermining America's moral authority and credibility as a champion of democracy and human rights. The failure to plan for post-war reconstruction and governance, coupled with widespread corruption and mismanagement, hindered efforts to stabilize Iraq and restore basic services, fueling resentment and disillusionment among Iraqis and exacerbating anti-American sentiment.

Furthermore, the Iraq War strained relations between the United States and its allies, particularly in Europe, where opposition to the war was widespread and vocal. The decision to bypass the United Nations and launch a unilateral military invasion of Iraq without a clear mandate or legal justification undermined the norms of international law and diplomacy, eroding trust and cooperation between the United States and key allies and partners.

The Iraq War also had broader implications for global perceptions of U.S. foreign policy and leadership, tarnishing America's reputation as a beacon of democracy and freedom and fueling perceptions of American imperialism and hegemony. The failure to uncover weapons of mass destruction in Iraq and the protracted and costly military occupation that followed raised serious questions about the wisdom and legitimacy of the Bush administration's interventionist policies and preemptive war doctrine, undermining America's moral authority and soft power on the world stage.

In conclusion, the invasion of Iraq in 2003 represented a defining moment in American foreign policy, with far-reaching consequences for regional stability and global perceptions of U.S. leadership and credibility. While the Bush administration presented several justifications for the war, including concerns about WMD proliferation, the promotion of democracy, and the fight against terrorism, the decision to invade Iraq remains deeply controversial and divisive, raising profound questions about the use of force, the limits of executive power, and the moral and strategic imperatives of U.S. interventionism in the post-9/11 world. As we shall explore in subsequent chapters, the legacy of the Iraq War continues to shape America's role in the Middle East and its approach to global conflict and security in the 21st century, underscoring the enduring complexities and uncertainties of the modern world order.

Chapter 6: The Global War on Terror

Evolution of the War on Terror as a Global Military Campaign:

The concept of the "War on Terror" emerged in the aftermath of the September 11, 2001, terrorist attacks as a rallying cry for a comprehensive and coordinated global effort to combat terrorism in all its forms. Spearheaded by the United States under the leadership of President George W. Bush, the War on Terror represented a paradigm shift in international security policy, prioritizing preemptive military action, intelligence sharing, and counterterrorism cooperation among nations.

The early phase of the War on Terror focused primarily on targeting Al-Qaeda and its affiliates, as well as the Taliban regime in Afghanistan, which provided sanctuary to the terrorist network responsible for the 9/11 attacks. The U.S.-led invasion of Afghanistan in October 2001, under the banner of Operation Enduring Freedom, sought to dismantle Al-Qaeda's operational infrastructure, remove the Taliban from power, and deny terrorist groups a safe haven from which to plan and launch future attacks.

Following the successful overthrow of the Taliban regime in Afghanistan, the War on Terror expanded to other theaters of operation, including Iraq, where the Bush administration justified military intervention on the grounds of eliminating weapons of mass destruction (WMDs), removing Saddam Hussein from power, and promoting democracy and stability in the Middle East. The invasion of Iraq in March 2003, under the pretext of preemptive self-defense and regime change, further expanded the scope and scale of the global conflict against terrorism.

In addition to military operations, the War on Terror encompassed a wide range of counterterrorism measures, including intelligence gathering, surveillance, financial sanctions, and law enforcement cooperation, aimed at disrupting terrorist networks, thwarting attacks, and apprehending or eliminating high-value targets. The establishment of the Department of Homeland Security, the enactment of the USA PATRIOT Act, and the implementation of enhanced security measures at home and abroad reflected the U.S. government's commitment to preventing future terrorist attacks and safeguarding the homeland.

Multinational Efforts to Combat Terrorism:

The War on Terror mobilized a broad coalition of nations committed to combating terrorism and upholding international peace and security. Recognizing the transnational nature of the terrorist threat and the need for collective action, the United States sought to build and maintain partnerships with allies and partners around the world, fostering cooperation in intelligence sharing, law enforcement, border security, and military operations.

NATO played a central role in the multinational efforts to combat terrorism, invoking Article 5 of its founding treaty for the first time in its history in response to the 9/11 attacks, declaring that an attack against one member state constituted an attack against all. NATO allies contributed troops and resources to the U.S.-led military campaigns in Afghanistan and Iraq, as well as to broader counterterrorism operations, including maritime patrols, air surveillance, and capacity-building initiatives in partner countries.

Moreover, regional organizations such as the European Union, the Arab League, and the African Union also played important roles in coordinating and supporting counterterrorism efforts within their respective spheres of influence. Through initiatives like the EU Counter-Terrorism Strategy and the African Union's Peace and Security Council, regional actors sought to strengthen cooperation among member states, enhance border security, and address the root causes of terrorism, including poverty, marginalization, and political instability.

Furthermore, international institutions like the United Nations played a vital role in providing a forum for diplomatic dialogue, conflict resolution, and peacekeeping operations in conflict-affected regions, including Afghanistan and Iraq. UN Security Council resolutions, such as Resolution 1373 and Resolution 1540, established legal frameworks for combating terrorism and preventing the proliferation of weapons of mass destruction, while UN peacekeeping missions provided critical support for post-conflict stabilization and reconstruction efforts in countries emerging from conflict.

Critiques and Controversies Surrounding the War on

Terror Strategy:

Despite its stated goals and objectives, the War on Terror strategy has been subject to numerous critiques and controversies, both domestically and internationally, regarding its effectiveness, legality, and human rights implications. Critics argue that the U.S.-led military interventions in Afghanistan and Iraq, as well as the broader counterterrorism measures implemented at home and abroad, have failed to achieve their stated objectives and have instead fueled instability, extremism, and resentment towards the United States.

One of the primary critiques of the War on Terror is its reliance on military force and unilateralism as the primary means of combating terrorism, often at the expense of diplomatic engagement, conflict prevention, and multilateral cooperation. The Bush administration's doctrine of preemptive war and regime change, exemplified by the invasion of Iraq, undermined international norms of sovereignty and non-interference and strained relations with key allies and partners, eroding trust and cooperation in the fight against terrorism.

Moreover, the War on Terror has been criticized for its broad and expansive definition of terrorism, which has been used to justify the targeting of political dissent, civil liberties, and minority communities under the guise of national security. The use of enhanced interrogation techniques, rendition, and indefinite detention without trial, as well as the expansion of surveillance powers and the erosion of privacy rights, have raised serious concerns about human rights abuses and violations of international law.

Furthermore, the War on Terror has been accused of exacerbating root causes of terrorism, including poverty, marginalization, and political repression, by fueling resentment and radicalization among affected populations. The civilian casualties, displacement, and destruction caused by military operations and counterterrorism measures have alienated local communities, strengthened insurgent groups, and undermined efforts to win hearts and minds and build sustainable peace and stability in conflict-affected regions.

In conclusion, the War on Terror represents a complex and multifaceted global campaign to combat terrorism in all its forms, encompassing military operations, intelligence sharing, law enforcement cooperation, and diplomatic engagement. While the War on Terror has achieved some successes in disrupting terrorist networks and preventing attacks, it has also been subject to critiques and controversies regarding its effectiveness, legality, and human rights implications. As we shall explore in subsequent chapters, the legacy of the War on Terror continues to shape America's approach to global conflict and security in the 21st century, underscoring the enduring challenges and complexities of combating terrorism in an interconnected and volatile world.

Chapter 7: Homeland Security and Domestic Surveillance

Establishment of the Department of Homeland Security:

In response to the September 11, 2001, terrorist attacks, the United States government underwent a significant reorganization of its national security apparatus, culminating in the creation of the Department of Homeland Security (DHS). Signed into law by President George W. Bush on November 25, 2002, the DHS brought together 22 federal agencies and departments under a single umbrella with the overarching mission of protecting the homeland from terrorist threats and other hazards.

The establishment of the DHS represented a watershed moment in American history, marking the most significant reorganization of the federal government since the creation of the Department of Defense in 1947. The consolidation of disparate agencies and functions, including border security, immigration enforcement, emergency management, and intelligence analysis, aimed to enhance coordination, communication, and collaboration among federal, state, and local stakeholders in the homeland security enterprise.

Led by its first Secretary, Tom Ridge, the DHS prioritized the development and implementation of a comprehensive and integrated strategy to detect, deter, and respond to terrorist threats and other homeland security challenges. The department's responsibilities encompassed a wide range of functions, including securing the nation's borders, ports, and transportation systems; protecting critical infrastructure and key assets; responding to natural disasters and other emergencies; and coordinating intelligence and information sharing efforts.

Implementation of Surveillance Measures and Counterterrorism Policies within the United States:

In the aftermath of the 9/11 attacks, the United States government implemented a series of surveillance measures and counterterrorism policies aimed at preventing future attacks and disrupting terrorist plots on American soil. These measures encompassed a broad spectrum of activities, ranging from enhanced intelligence gathering and law enforcement capabilities to expanded security screening and monitoring of individuals and communities deemed to be at risk of radicalization or involvement in terrorist activities.

One of the most controversial and far-reaching surveillance programs implemented by the U.S. government in the wake of 9/11 was the National Security Agency's (NSA) warrantless wiretapping program, authorized by President Bush shortly after the attacks. Under this program, known as the Terrorist Surveillance Program (TSP), the NSA conducted warrantless surveillance of international communications involving U.S. persons suspected of having ties to terrorist organizations, circumventing traditional legal safeguards and oversight mechanisms.

In addition to the TSP, the USA PATRIOT Act, enacted by Congress in October 2001, significantly expanded the government's surveillance and investigative powers, granting law enforcement agencies broader authority to conduct surveillance, obtain electronic communications records, and detain suspected terrorists without due process. The PATRIOT Act also facilitated information sharing between law enforcement and intelligence agencies and enhanced penalties for terrorist offenses and material support for terrorism.

Furthermore, the creation of fusion centers, joint terrorism task forces, and other multi-agency coordination mechanisms at the federal, state, and local levels facilitated the sharing of intelligence and information between law enforcement, intelligence, and homeland security agencies, enabling a more proactive and integrated approach to detecting and disrupting terrorist threats within the United States.

Balancing National Security with Civil Liberties:

The implementation of surveillance measures and counterterrorism policies within the United States raised significant concerns about the balance between national security imperatives and civil liberties protections, particularly with regard to privacy rights, due process, and freedom of expression. Critics argued that the expansion of government surveillance powers and the erosion of constitutional safeguards undermined fundamental principles of democracy and individual rights, threatening to erode the very freedoms that terrorists sought to undermine.

The NSA's warrantless wiretapping program, in particular, sparked heated debate and legal challenges over its legality and constitutionality, with critics contending that the program violated the Fourth Amendment's protection against unreasonable searches and seizures and the Foreign Intelligence Surveillance Act (FISA), which established procedures for obtaining warrants for electronic surveillance of foreign intelligence targets.

Similarly, provisions of the USA PATRIOT Act granting the government expanded authority to conduct surveillance, obtain records, and detain suspects without adequate judicial oversight raised concerns about potential abuses of power and violations of due process rights. Critics argued that the broad and ambiguous language of the PATRIOT Act could be interpreted in ways that infringed on civil liberties and marginalized vulnerable communities, including immigrants, Muslims, and political dissidents.

Moreover, the targeting of specific ethnic and religious communities for surveillance and profiling, as well as the use of discriminatory practices such as racial and religious profiling, exacerbated tensions and mistrust between law enforcement agencies and minority communities, undermining efforts to build trust and cooperation in the fight against terrorism.

In response to these concerns, civil liberties advocates, legal scholars, and grassroots activists mobilized to challenge and reform surveillance practices and counterterrorism policies perceived to be unconstitutional or discriminatory. Legal challenges to the NSA's warrantless wiretapping program, congressional oversight hearings on the PATRIOT Act, and public advocacy campaigns calling for greater transparency and accountability in government surveillance programs helped to raise awareness and pressure policymakers to enact reforms.

In conclusion, the establishment of the Department of Homeland Security and the implementation of surveillance measures and counterterrorism policies within the United States in the aftermath of the 9/11 attacks represented a delicate balancing act between national security imperatives and civil liberties protections. While these measures were intended to enhance the government's ability to detect, deter, and respond to terrorist threats, they also raised significant concerns about privacy rights, due process, and freedom of expression. As we shall explore in subsequent chapters, the debate over the proper balance between security and liberty continues to shape America's approach to homeland security and counterterrorism in the 21st century, underscoring the enduring tensions between the imperatives of national security and the rights and freedoms guaranteed by the Constitution.

Chapter 8: Interrogation and Detention

Discussion of Enhanced Interrogation Techniques and Detention Policies:

In the aftermath of the September 11, 2001, terrorist attacks, the United States government implemented a series of controversial interrogation and detention policies aimed at extracting intelligence from suspected terrorists and preventing future attacks. These policies, which included the use of enhanced interrogation techniques (EITs) and the indefinite detention of suspected terrorists without trial, sparked intense legal, ethical, and moral debates both domestically and internationally.

Enhanced interrogation techniques, also known as "harsh" or "enhanced" interrogation methods, encompassed a range of coercive and aggressive interrogation tactics designed to break the will of detainees and compel them to provide valuable intelligence information. These techniques, which included waterboarding, stress positions, sleep deprivation, sensory deprivation, and physical abuse, were justified by proponents as necessary and effective means of extracting actionable intelligence from high-value detainees.

The use of enhanced interrogation techniques was authorized by senior officials in the Bush administration, including President George W. Bush and his top advisors, who argued that such methods were necessary to extract information from suspected terrorists who posed a grave and imminent threat to national security. The CIA, in particular, played a central role in implementing and overseeing the use of EITs against detainees held in secret prisons, known as "black sites," around the world.

In addition to enhanced interrogation techniques, the U.S. government implemented a policy of indefinite detention for suspected terrorists captured in the global war on terror. Under this policy, individuals deemed to be "enemy combatants" or "unlawful enemy combatants" were held indefinitely without charge or trial, often in extrajudicial detention facilities such as Guantanamo Bay detention camp in Cuba, where they were denied access to legal representation and due process rights.

Legal and Ethical Debates Surrounding the Treatment of Suspected Terrorists:

The use of enhanced interrogation techniques and the policy of indefinite detention of suspected terrorists sparked heated legal, ethical, and moral debates over the treatment of detainees and the adherence to international human rights norms and legal principles. Critics argued that the use of EITs, including waterboarding and other forms of torture, violated domestic and international laws prohibiting torture and cruel, inhuman, or degrading treatment, as well as fundamental principles of human dignity and morality.

Moreover, critics contended that the policy of indefinite detention without trial violated the constitutional right to due process and habeas corpus, which guarantees individuals the right to challenge the lawfulness of their detention before a neutral judicial authority. The detention of suspected terrorists without charge or trial, often based on classified or dubious intelligence information, raised serious concerns about arbitrary detention, lack of accountability, and the erosion of the rule of law.

In response to these concerns, human rights organizations, legal advocacy groups, and civil liberties advocates mobilized to challenge and reform the U.S. government's interrogation and detention policies, calling for greater transparency, accountability, and adherence to international human rights standards. Legal challenges to the use of enhanced interrogation techniques and the policy of indefinite detention, as well as public advocacy campaigns and congressional oversight hearings, helped to raise awareness and pressure policymakers to enact reforms.

Furthermore, the release of classified documents, investigative reports, and testimonies from former detainees and interrogators shed light on the extent and nature of the abuses perpetrated in the name of national security, fueling public outrage and condemnation both domestically and internationally. The revelations of torture and mistreatment at Abu Ghraib prison in Iraq, Guantanamo Bay detention camp, and other detention facilities tarnished America's reputation as a champion of human rights and democratic values, undermining U.S. credibility and moral authority on the world stage.

Impact on U.S. Credibility and International Human

Rights Norms:

The use of enhanced interrogation techniques and the policy of indefinite detention of suspected terrorists had profound and lasting consequences for U.S. credibility and international human rights norms, undermining America's reputation as a leader in the promotion of democracy, freedom, and human rights. The revelations of torture and abuse perpetrated by U.S. personnel against detainees, including documented cases of waterboarding, sleep deprivation, and physical violence, shocked the conscience of the international community and sparked condemnation from human rights organizations, foreign governments, and international bodies.

Moreover, the policy of indefinite detention without trial at Guantanamo Bay and other detention facilities symbolized a departure from established legal norms and principles of due process and undermined the United States' credibility as a defender of the rule of law and individual rights. The prolonged detention of individuals without charge or trial, often based on vague or unsubstantiated allegations of terrorism, raised serious concerns about arbitrary detention, lack of transparency, and the erosion of constitutional rights.

Furthermore, the use of enhanced interrogation techniques and the policy of indefinite detention of suspected terrorists fueled anti-American sentiment and propaganda by terrorist organizations and extremist groups, who exploited the perceived hypocrisy and moral contradictions of U.S. counterterrorism policies to recruit new followers and justify their own acts of violence and extremism. The erosion of trust and goodwill towards the United States among key allies and partners, particularly in Europe and the Middle East, further undermined America's ability to build consensus and cooperation in the global fight against terrorism.

In conclusion, the use of enhanced interrogation techniques and the policy of indefinite detention of suspected terrorists in the aftermath of the September 11, 2001, terrorist attacks represented a profound departure from established legal norms and ethical principles, raising serious concerns about human rights abuses and violations of international law. The debates and controversies surrounding the treatment of detainees underscored the challenges of balancing national security imperatives with respect for civil liberties and human rights, and the enduring tensions between security and liberty in the context of the global war on terror. As we shall explore in subsequent chapters, the legacy of the interrogation and detention policies continues to shape America's approach to counterterrorism and national security in the 21st century, underscoring the complexities and moral dilemmas inherent in the pursuit of security in an uncertain and dangerous world.

Chapter 9: The Obama Era: Shifting Strategies

Examination of President Barack Obama's Approach to Counterterrorism:

The election of Barack Obama as the 44th President of the United States in 2008 marked a significant shift in American foreign policy and counterterrorism strategy. Building on the legacy of his predecessor, President George W. Bush, Obama inherited a nation grappling with the aftermath of the September 11, 2001, terrorist attacks and engaged in a protracted and costly global war on terror. However, Obama sought to chart a new course for U.S. counterterrorism efforts, emphasizing a more pragmatic and nuanced approach that prioritized diplomacy, multilateralism, and international cooperation while seeking to uphold American values and principles.

From the outset of his presidency, Obama made it clear that he intended to recalibrate America's approach to counterterrorism, moving away from the unilateralism and interventionism of the Bush years towards a more balanced and sustainable strategy grounded in the rule of law, respect for human rights, and engagement with the international community. Recognizing the limitations and costs of military force as a tool of counterterrorism, Obama sought to leverage a broader array of instruments, including diplomacy, development assistance, and intelligence cooperation, to address the underlying drivers of extremism and violence.

One of the hallmarks of Obama's approach to counterterrorism was his commitment to closing the Guantanamo Bay detention camp, which had come to symbolize the excesses and abuses of the post-9/11 era. Despite facing significant political and legal obstacles, Obama issued an executive order on his second day in office mandating the closure of Guantanamo and the review of detention policies, signaling his administration's commitment to restoring the rule of law and due process rights for detainees.

Moreover, Obama sought to redefine America's role in the world and repair strained relations with key allies and partners, particularly in Europe and the Muslim world, by reaffirming America's commitment to international law, human rights, and democratic values. Through initiatives like the New START

Treaty with Russia, the Iran nuclear deal, and the Paris Agreement on climate change, Obama sought to demonstrate America's willingness to engage in constructive diplomacy and dialogue to address global challenges and promote peace and stability.

Transition from the Bush Doctrine to a More Nuanced Strategy:

The Obama administration's approach to counterterrorism represented a departure from the Bush Doctrine of preemptive war and unilateralism towards a more nuanced and pragmatic strategy that sought to strike a balance between security imperatives and respect for civil liberties and human rights. While Obama inherited a robust counterterrorism infrastructure and toolkit from the Bush administration, including drone warfare and targeted killings, he sought to reorient these tools within a broader framework of legal and ethical constraints.

One of the key pillars of Obama's counterterrorism strategy was his emphasis on the use of targeted drone strikes as a means of disrupting terrorist networks and eliminating high-value targets while minimizing civilian casualties and collateral damage. Under Obama's watch, the use of unmanned aerial vehicles (UAVs), or drones, for targeted killings expanded significantly, with strikes conducted in countries such as Pakistan, Yemen, Somalia, and Libya against suspected terrorists affiliated with groups like Al-Qaeda and its affiliates.

The use of drones for targeted killings represented a controversial and contentious aspect of Obama's counterterrorism policy, raising serious legal, ethical, and moral questions about the legality and legitimacy of extrajudicial killings, the accuracy of targeting algorithms, and the risk of civilian harm. Critics argued that the use of drones for targeted killings violated international law, including the laws of armed conflict and human rights law, and undermined principles of accountability, transparency, and due process.

Moreover, the reliance on drone warfare as a primary tool of counterterrorism risked perpetuating a cycle of violence and radicalization, alienating local populations, and undermining America's credibility and legitimacy in the eyes of the world. The lack of transparency and accountability surrounding drone strikes, including the absence of public disclosure of casualty figures and the criteria for targeting decisions, fueled mistrust and suspicion among affected communities and human rights organizations.

However, proponents of drone warfare argued that it represented a precise and effective means of targeting terrorists while minimizing the risk to U.S. personnel and reducing the need for large-scale military interventions. They contended that drones offered a unique capability to strike terrorists in remote and inaccessible areas, disrupt their operations, and degrade their ability to plan and launch attacks against the United States and its allies.

Furthermore, the Obama administration sought to mitigate the risks and challenges associated with drone warfare by implementing stricter guidelines and oversight mechanisms governing the use of drones for targeted killings. In 2013, Obama issued a presidential policy guidance (PPG) establishing clear criteria and procedures for drone strikes, including the requirement of near-certainty that the target posed an imminent threat to the United States and the minimization of civilian casualties.

Impact on U.S. Credibility and International Human Rights Norms:

The use of drones for targeted killings under the Obama administration had profound and far-reaching consequences for U.S. credibility, moral authority, and adherence to international human rights norms. While Obama sought to portray drone warfare as a more precise and humane alternative to traditional military interventions, the secrecy surrounding drone strikes and the lack of transparency and accountability undermined America's credibility and legitimacy in the eyes of the world.

The absence of clear legal frameworks and judicial oversight mechanisms governing the use of drones for targeted killings raised serious concerns about the legality and legitimacy of such operations under international law. Human rights organizations, legal experts, and civil liberties advocates called for greater transparency, accountability, and adherence to international legal standards, including the requirement of proportionality, necessity, and distinction in the conduct of armed conflict.

Moreover, the use of drones for targeted killings risked setting dangerous precedents and undermining established norms of sovereignty, territorial integrity, and the right to life. The expansion of the U.S. drone program to countries like Pakistan, Yemen, and Somalia without the consent or authorization of the host governments raised serious questions about the legality of extraterritorial targeted killings and the implications for state sovereignty and the rule of law.

Furthermore, the reliance on drone warfare as a primary tool of counterterrorism risked perpetuating a cycle of violence and radicalization, fueling anti-American sentiment and recruitment by terrorist organizations. The unintended consequences of drone strikes, including civilian casualties, displacement, and psychological trauma, fueled resentment and anger among affected communities, undermining America's efforts to win hearts and minds and build trust and cooperation in the fight against terrorism.

In conclusion, the Obama administration's approach to counterterrorism represented a significant departure from the Bush era's unilateralism and interventionism towards a more nuanced and pragmatic strategy grounded in diplomacy, multilateralism, and respect for human rights. However, the use of drones for targeted killings emerged as a controversial and contentious aspect of Obama's counterterrorism policy, raising serious legal, ethical, and moral questions about the legality and legitimacy of extrajudicial killings and the impact on U.S. credibility and international human rights norms. As we shall explore in subsequent chapters, the legacy of Obama's counterterrorism strategy continues to shape America's approach to global conflict and security in the 21st century, underscoring the enduring complexities and moral dilemmas inherent in the pursuit of security in an interconnected and volatile world.

Chapter 10: The Arab Spring and its Aftermath

Analysis of the Arab Spring Uprisings and Their Implications for Counterterrorism Efforts:

The Arab Spring, a series of pro-democracy uprisings that swept across the Middle East and North Africa in the early 2010s, represented a seismic shift in the political landscape of the region and posed significant challenges for counterterrorism efforts. Sparked by widespread grievances over corruption, authoritarian rule, economic inequality, and lack of political freedoms, the Arab Spring uprisings unleashed popular movements demanding political reform, social justice, and democratic governance.

The Arab Spring began in December 2010 with the self-immolation of Tunisian street vendor Mohamed Bouazizi in protest against government corruption and police brutality, which ignited mass protests and demonstrations across Tunisia and eventually led to the overthrow of President Zine El Abidine Ben Ali in January 2011. The success of the Tunisian revolution inspired similar movements in countries like Egypt, Libya, Syria, Yemen, Bahrain, and beyond, as millions of people took to the streets to demand change and challenge entrenched authoritarian regimes.

The implications of the Arab Spring for counterterrorism efforts were profound and multifaceted. On one hand, the uprisings represented a repudiation of the status quo and a rejection of autocratic rule and repression, which had fueled grievances and resentment and provided fertile ground for extremist ideologies to take root. The democratic aspirations and demands for accountability and transparency expressed by protesters resonated with many disillusioned with the authoritarian regimes that had long dominated the region.

However, the Arab Spring also created fertile ground for the proliferation of extremist groups and terrorist organizations seeking to exploit power vacuums, societal instability, and sectarian divisions for their own ends. In countries like Libya, Syria, and Yemen, where the uprisings descended into protracted civil wars and violent conflict, extremist groups like Al-Qaeda, ISIS, and their affiliates capitalized on the chaos and insecurity to expand their influence, establish safe havens, and recruit fighters.

Destabilization of the Middle East and Rise of ISIS:

The destabilization unleashed by the Arab Spring uprisings, coupled with long-standing grievances and regional power struggles, created fertile ground for the rise of ISIS (Islamic State of Iraq and Syria), also known as ISIL (Islamic State of Iraq and the Levant), as a potent and formidable terrorist organization. Born out of the remnants of Al-Qaeda in Iraq and the Syrian civil war, ISIS emerged as a transnational jihadist movement committed to establishing a self-styled caliphate based on its radical interpretation of Islamic law.

The rise of ISIS represented a significant escalation in the threat posed by terrorist groups in the Middle East and beyond, as the organization seized large swathes of territory in Iraq and Syria, imposed brutal and draconian rule on the populations under its control, and carried out a campaign of terror and violence aimed at sowing chaos, instilling fear, and imposing its extremist ideology on others. The group's sophisticated propaganda and social media savvy enabled it to attract tens of thousands of foreign fighters from around the world, including Europe, North America, and beyond, to join its ranks.

The emergence of ISIS as a formidable terrorist organization posed profound challenges for counterterrorism efforts, as the group's territorial control, military capabilities, and transnational reach posed a direct threat to regional stability, international security, and the values of democracy, human rights, and pluralism. The group's ruthless tactics, including mass executions, beheadings, and sexual slavery, shocked the world and galvanized global efforts to confront and defeat the ISIS threat.

In response to the rise of ISIS, the United States and its allies launched a multinational military campaign, known as Operation Inherent Resolve, to degrade and defeat the terrorist group and its affiliates in Iraq and Syria. Through a combination of airstrikes, special operations raids, and support for local partners, including the Iraqi security forces and Kurdish Peshmerga fighters in Iraq and the Syrian Democratic Forces (SDF) in Syria, the coalition succeeded in reclaiming significant territory from ISIS and dismantling its organizational infrastructure.

Challenges Posed by Non-State Actors in the Post-Arab Spring Era:

The Arab Spring and its aftermath unleashed a wave of instability, violence, and conflict across the Middle East and North Africa, creating fertile ground for the proliferation of non-state actors, extremist groups, and terrorist organizations seeking to exploit power vacuums and societal divisions for their own ends. In addition to ISIS, a myriad of other extremist groups and militias emerged in countries like Libya, Syria, Yemen, and beyond, challenging the authority of central governments, undermining state institutions, and perpetuating cycles of violence and instability.

One of the key challenges posed by non-state actors in the post-Arab Spring era was the erosion of state sovereignty and territorial integrity, as armed groups and extremist organizations established de facto control over vast swaths of territory, challenged the authority of central governments, and imposed their own rule and governance structures on the populations under their control. In countries like Syria and Yemen, where state institutions were weakened or fragmented by conflict, non-state actors filled the void, providing essential services, administering justice, and imposing their own interpretation of Islamic law.

Moreover, the proliferation of non-state actors and extremist groups in the wake of the Arab Spring exacerbated sectarian tensions, fueled communal violence, and deepened divisions within societies already grappling with political upheaval and economic hardship. The rise of sectarian militias and armed factions, particularly in countries like Iraq and Syria, further polarized communities along ethnic, religious, and tribal lines, exacerbating social cleavages and hindering efforts at reconciliation and conflict resolution.

Furthermore, the presence of non-state actors and extremist groups in conflict-affected regions posed significant challenges for humanitarian organizations and aid agencies seeking to deliver assistance and support to vulnerable populations. Humanitarian access was often restricted or blocked by armed groups, endangering the lives and livelihoods of civilians trapped in conflict zones and exacerbating humanitarian crises, including food insecurity, displacement, and lack of access to essential services like healthcare and education.

In conclusion, the Arab Spring and its aftermath unleashed a wave of instability, violence, and conflict across the Middle East and North Africa, creating fertile ground for the rise of non-state actors, extremist groups, and terrorist organizations seeking to exploit power vacuums and societal divisions for their own ends. The proliferation of non-state actors, including ISIS, posed profound challenges for regional stability, international security, and efforts to promote democracy, human rights, and the rule of law. As we shall explore in subsequent chapters, the legacy of the Arab Spring continues to shape America's approach to global conflict and security in the 21st century, underscoring the enduring complexities and challenges of addressing the root causes of extremism and violence in an increasingly interconnected and volatile world.

Chapter 11: The Islamic State (ISIS) Threat

Emergence and Expansion of ISIS in Iraq and Syria:

The emergence and expansion of the Islamic State of Iraq and Syria (ISIS) represented a significant and unprecedented threat to regional stability, international security, and the values of democracy, human rights, and pluralism. Born out of the chaos and instability unleashed by the Arab Spring uprisings and the sectarian tensions and power struggles that followed, ISIS emerged as a formidable terrorist organization committed to establishing a self-styled caliphate based on its radical interpretation of Islamic law.

The roots of ISIS can be traced back to the aftermath of the 2003 U.S.-led invasion of Iraq and the subsequent collapse of the Ba'athist regime led by Saddam Hussein. The power vacuum and sectarian tensions that followed the fall of Saddam's regime created fertile ground for the emergence of extremist groups and militias, including Al-Qaeda in Iraq (AQI), which later rebranded itself as the Islamic State of Iraq (ISI) under the leadership of Abu Musab al-Zarqawi.

Under Zarqawi's leadership, ISI waged a brutal campaign of terror and violence against Iraqi civilians, security forces, and U.S. military personnel, seeking to incite sectarian conflict and undermine efforts to stabilize and rebuild Iraq. The group's tactics, which included suicide bombings, assassinations, and mass casualty attacks, fueled resentment and anger among Iraq's Sunni Arab population, who felt marginalized and disenfranchised by the country's Shiite-dominated government.

However, it was not until the outbreak of the Syrian civil war in 2011 that ISIS was able to expand its operations and establish a foothold in neighboring Syria. Taking advantage of the power vacuum created by the collapse of the Assad regime's control over large parts of the country, ISIS seized territory in eastern Syria and declared the establishment of a caliphate, or Islamic state, in June 2014, with its leader Abu Bakr al-Baghdadi proclaiming himself the caliph.

The rapid expansion of ISIS in Iraq and Syria sent shockwaves throughout the region and the world, as the group seized control of major cities, including Mosul, Iraq's second-largest city, and Raqqa, the de facto capital of its self-proclaimed caliphate. ISIS imposed its brutal and draconian rule on the populations under its control, enforcing strict Islamic law, carrying out public executions, imposing taxes and fees on residents, and committing widespread human rights abuses.

Response of the United States and its Allies to the ISIS Threat:

The emergence of ISIS as a formidable terrorist organization and the establishment of its self-styled caliphate in Iraq and Syria posed a direct threat to regional stability, international security, and the values of democracy, human rights, and pluralism. In response to the ISIS threat, the United States and its allies launched a multinational military campaign aimed at degrading and defeating the terrorist group and its affiliates.

Operation Inherent Resolve, the U.S.-led military campaign against ISIS, was launched in August 2014 with the aim of dismantling the terrorist group's organizational infrastructure, denying it safe haven, and liberating territory under its control in Iraq and Syria. The coalition, which comprised more than 80 countries, including NATO allies, Arab states, and regional partners, employed a combination of airstrikes, special operations raids, and support for local partners on the ground to achieve its objectives.

The United States played a leading role in the coalition's military efforts, conducting thousands of airstrikes against ISIS targets in Iraq and Syria and providing training, equipment, and support to local forces, including the Iraqi security forces, Kurdish Peshmerga fighters, and the Syrian Democratic Forces (SDF). U.S. Special Operations Forces also conducted targeted raids against high-value ISIS targets, including senior leaders and operatives, in coordination with partner forces on the ground.

In addition to military action, the coalition also sought to undermine ISIS's propaganda and recruitment efforts, disrupt its financing and logistics networks, and counter its extremist ideology through diplomatic, economic, and information warfare measures. Efforts to counter ISIS's online presence and social media savvy, which enabled the group to attract tens of thousands of foreign fighters from around the world, became an increasingly important aspect of the coalition's strategy.

Furthermore, the coalition worked to address the underlying drivers of extremism and violence in Iraq and Syria, including political instability, economic hardship, sectarian tensions, and governance failures, through support for stabilization and reconstruction efforts, capacity-building initiatives, and diplomatic engagement with local actors. Efforts to promote inclusive governance, reconciliation, and the rule of law were seen as essential components of the long-term strategy to prevent the resurgence of extremist groups like ISIS.

Strategies Employed to Degrade and Defeat ISIS:

The coalition's strategy to degrade and defeat ISIS in Iraq and Syria involved a multi-faceted and comprehensive approach that combined military, diplomatic, economic, and informational elements. Key components of the strategy included:

1. Military Operations: The coalition conducted a relentless campaign of airstrikes against ISIS targets in Iraq and Syria, targeting command and control centers, weapons depots, training camps, and infrastructure. Special Operations Forces also conducted targeted raids against high-value ISIS targets, including senior leaders and operatives. The coalition provided training, equipment, and support to local forces, including the Iraqi security forces, Kurdish Peshmerga fighters, and the Syrian Democratic Forces (SDF), to enable them to conduct ground operations against ISIS militants and reclaim territory under the group's control.

2. Counterterrorism and Intelligence Cooperation: The coalition worked to enhance intelligence sharing and coordination among member states, improve border security and counterterrorism capabilities, and disrupt ISIS's financing and logistics networks. Efforts to counter ISIS's propaganda and recruitment efforts, including through online counter-messaging campaigns and engagement with local communities, were also prioritized.

3. Stabilization and Reconstruction: The coalition supported stabilization and reconstruction efforts in areas liberated from ISIS control, including the provision of humanitarian assistance, restoration of essential services, and reconstruction of critical infrastructure. Efforts to promote inclusive governance, reconciliation, and the rule of law were aimed at addressing the underlying

grievances that had fueled support for ISIS and preventing the group's resurgence.

4. Diplomatic Engagement: The coalition engaged in diplomatic efforts to build consensus and cooperation among member states, regional actors, and international partners in the fight against ISIS. Diplomatic initiatives aimed at addressing the political and security challenges in Iraq and Syria, including efforts to resolve conflicts and promote political dialogue, were seen as essential for achieving lasting peace and stability in the region.

5. Economic Pressure: The coalition implemented measures to disrupt ISIS's financing and economic resources, including targeted sanctions, asset freezes, and efforts to interdict illicit financial flows. Economic incentives and support for local communities were also employed to undercut support for ISIS and deprive the group of recruitment and financing opportunities.

Overall, the coalition's strategy to degrade and defeat ISIS in Iraq and Syria achieved significant success in reclaiming territory, dismantling the group's organizational infrastructure, and reducing its operational capabilities. However, the threat posed by ISIS remains far from eradicated, as the group continues to adapt and evolve in response to military pressure and exploit opportunities for recruitment and expansion in conflict-affected regions. As we shall explore in subsequent chapters, the legacy of the ISIS threat continues to shape America's approach to global conflict and security in the 21st century, underscoring the enduring challenges and complexities of combating terrorism in an interconnected and volatile world.

Chapter 12: Cyber Warfare and Terrorism

Exploration of the Intersection between Cyber Warfare and Terrorism:

The emergence of the digital age has transformed the nature of warfare and terrorism, ushering in an era of cyber warfare where conflicts are waged not only on physical battlefields but also in the virtual realm of cyberspace. The intersection between cyber warfare and terrorism has created new challenges and opportunities for non-state actors, extremist groups, and state-sponsored actors seeking to advance their strategic objectives, undermine their adversaries, and inflict harm on civilian populations.

Cyber warfare refers to the use of digital technologies, including computers, networks, and the internet, to conduct military operations, espionage, sabotage, and subversion in support of strategic objectives. While traditionally associated with state actors and military organizations, cyber warfare has increasingly become a tool of choice for non-state actors, including terrorist groups, insurgent movements, and criminal organizations, seeking to exploit vulnerabilities in cyberspace to advance their agendas and achieve their goals.

Terrorist groups and extremist organizations have demonstrated a growing interest in exploiting cyberspace for propaganda, recruitment, fundraising, and operational planning purposes. From spreading extremist ideologies and inciting violence to recruiting new followers and coordinating attacks, terrorist groups have leveraged social media platforms, encrypted messaging apps, and online forums to amplify their message, radicalize vulnerable individuals, and mobilize supporters around the world.

Moreover, terrorist groups have also sought to harness the disruptive potential of cyber attacks to inflict harm on their adversaries, disrupt critical infrastructure, and undermine public confidence in government institutions and security apparatuses. While the capabilities of terrorist groups in the cyber domain may be limited compared to those of state-sponsored actors, the asymmetric nature of cyber warfare means that even relatively low-level attacks can have significant disruptive and destabilizing effects.

Cyber Attacks as a Tool of Non-State Actors and State-Sponsored Terrorism:

The use of cyber attacks as a tool of non-state actors and state-sponsored terrorism represents a growing threat to international security, as advances in technology and connectivity have expanded the capabilities and reach of malicious actors operating in cyberspace. While state-sponsored cyber attacks have traditionally been associated with espionage, sabotage, and geopolitical rivalries, the emergence of non-state actors, including terrorist groups and criminal organizations, has added a new dimension to the cyber threat landscape.

Terrorist groups have increasingly sought to exploit cyberspace to advance their strategic objectives, enhance their operational capabilities, and inflict harm on their adversaries. From conducting disruptive cyber attacks on critical infrastructure, such as power grids, transportation systems, and financial institutions, to launching propaganda campaigns and psychological operations aimed at spreading fear and undermining public confidence, terrorist groups have demonstrated a growing interest in leveraging the digital domain to achieve their goals.

One of the most significant cyber threats posed by terrorist groups is the potential for cyber attacks on critical infrastructure, such as energy, transportation, telecommunications, and healthcare systems, which are essential for the functioning of modern societies and economies. Disruptive cyber attacks on critical infrastructure could have catastrophic consequences, causing widespread disruption, economic damage, and loss of life, and undermining public safety and national security.

Moreover, terrorist groups have also sought to exploit cyberspace for propaganda, recruitment, and psychological warfare purposes, using social media platforms, encrypted messaging apps, and online forums to disseminate extremist ideologies, radicalize vulnerable individuals, and inspire or incite acts of violence. The anonymity and reach of the internet enable terrorist groups to reach a global audience and amplify their message, making it increasingly challenging for authorities to detect and disrupt their activities.

In addition to non-state actors, state-sponsored terrorism represents another significant threat in the cyber domain, as governments seek to leverage cyber attacks as a means of advancing their strategic interests, exerting influence, and undermining their adversaries. State-sponsored cyber attacks can take various forms, including espionage, sabotage, disinformation, and propaganda, and may target government agencies, military organizations, critical infrastructure, and private sector entities.

Efforts to Protect Critical Infrastructure and Combat Cyber Threats:

The growing threat posed by cyber warfare and terrorism has prompted governments, international organizations, and private sector entities to bolster their cybersecurity capabilities and enhance efforts to protect critical infrastructure, safeguard sensitive information, and combat cyber threats. While there is no silver bullet solution to the complex and evolving challenges posed by cyber attacks, a multi-faceted and holistic approach that combines technical, policy, and diplomatic measures is essential for effectively addressing the cyber threat landscape.

One of the key components of efforts to combat cyber threats is the development and implementation of robust cybersecurity measures and best practices to protect critical infrastructure and sensitive information from cyber attacks. This includes deploying firewalls, intrusion detection systems, encryption technologies, and other defensive mechanisms to detect and mitigate cyber threats, as well as conducting regular security audits and vulnerability assessments to identify and address weaknesses in systems and networks.

Moreover, enhancing cybersecurity awareness and education among government officials, private sector employees, and the general public is crucial for building a cyber-resilient society capable of recognizing and responding to cyber threats effectively. Training programs, awareness campaigns, and information sharing initiatives can help raise awareness about the risks and consequences of cyber attacks, promote good cyber hygiene practices, and empower individuals and organizations to protect themselves against cyber threats.

Furthermore, fostering international cooperation and collaboration is essential for effectively combating cyber threats and addressing the transnational nature of cyber warfare and terrorism. Information sharing, joint exercises, capacity-building initiatives, and diplomatic engagement can help strengthen cybersecurity capabilities, build trust and confidence among stakeholders, and facilitate coordinated responses to cyber incidents and threats.

In addition to technical measures, efforts to combat cyber threats also require robust legal frameworks, policies, and regulations to deter malicious actors, hold them accountable for their actions, and promote responsible behavior in cyberspace. International treaties, conventions, and norms, such as the United Nations Group of Governmental Experts (UNGGE) on Developments in the Field of Information and Telecommunications in the Context of International Security, provide a framework for guiding state behavior and promoting responsible conduct in cyberspace.

Moreover, law enforcement and intelligence agencies play a crucial role in investigating cyber crimes, disrupting cyber threats, and prosecuting individuals and groups engaged in malicious cyber activities. Cooperation between law enforcement agencies, intelligence services, and cybersecurity experts is essential for identifying and disrupting cyber threats, attributing attacks to their perpetrators, and holding them accountable for their actions.

In conclusion, the intersection between cyber warfare and terrorism represents a growing threat to international security, as advances in technology and connectivity have expanded the capabilities and reach of malicious actors operating in cyberspace. Efforts to protect critical infrastructure, combat cyber threats, and promote responsible behavior in cyberspace require a multi-faceted and holistic approach that combines technical, policy, and diplomatic measures. By strengthening cybersecurity capabilities, enhancing international cooperation, and promoting responsible conduct in cyberspace, stakeholders can work together to address the complex and evolving challenges posed by cyber warfare and terrorism in the 21st century.

Chapter 13: The Trump Administration's Approach

Assessment of President Donald Trump's Policies on Counterterrorism:

The presidency of Donald Trump brought a distinct approach to counterterrorism, characterized by a blend of continuity with previous administrations' strategies and notable departures in rhetoric and policy. Trump's policies on counterterrorism were shaped by his "America First" foreign policy doctrine, which prioritized national security, economic interests, and sovereignty, while advocating for a more transactional approach to international relations.

One of the key pillars of Trump's counterterrorism strategy was the aggressive pursuit of military force against terrorist groups, particularly ISIS. Trump vowed to "bomb the hell out of ISIS" during his campaign and subsequently authorized an escalation of U.S. military operations against the terrorist group in Iraq and Syria. Under Trump's leadership, the U.S.-led coalition intensified airstrikes, special operations raids, and support for local partners, resulting in the rapid degradation and territorial defeat of ISIS's self-proclaimed caliphate.

In addition to military action, Trump also prioritized efforts to enhance border security and restrict immigration from countries deemed to pose a terrorist threat. Trump's controversial travel bans, which targeted predominantly Muslim-majority countries, were framed as necessary measures to protect the United States from terrorist infiltration and to prevent the entry of individuals deemed to pose a risk to national security. However, critics argued that the bans were discriminatory and counterproductive, fueling anti-American sentiment and undermining U.S. credibility and leadership on the global stage.

Moreover, Trump's administration took steps to strengthen law enforcement and intelligence capabilities to counter domestic terrorism threats, including white supremacist extremism and far-right violence. Trump signed executive orders and allocated resources to combat domestic terrorism and extremism, although his administration faced criticism for downplaying the threat posed by far-right groups and failing to prioritize efforts to address the root causes of extremism and radicalization.

Continuity and Divergence from Previous Administrations' Strategies:

While Trump's counterterrorism policies represented a departure from the more interventionist and multilateral approach of previous administrations, particularly under President Barack Obama, they also reflected continuity in certain key areas, such as the prioritization of military force and intelligence cooperation. Trump's administration built upon the foundations laid by its predecessors, including the use of drone warfare, targeted killings, and special operations raids, as well as efforts to disrupt terrorist financing and propaganda networks.

At the same time, Trump's administration diverged from previous administrations' strategies in several significant ways, including its emphasis on unilateralism, transactional diplomacy, and the prioritization of short-term security objectives over long-term stability and human rights concerns. Trump's "America First" approach to foreign policy prioritized the protection of U.S. interests and the pursuit of narrow security objectives, often at the expense of broader diplomatic engagement and multilateral cooperation.

Moreover, Trump's administration adopted a more confrontational stance towards traditional allies and partners, challenging established norms and institutions, and seeking to renegotiate international agreements and alliances. Trump's criticism of NATO, the European Union, and other international organizations raised concerns about the erosion of transatlantic unity and cooperation in the fight against terrorism and other global challenges.

Impact of Trump's Rhetoric and Actions on Global Perceptions of the United States:

The rhetoric and actions of the Trump administration had a significant impact on global perceptions of the United States, shaping attitudes towards U.S. leadership, credibility, and commitment to values such as democracy, human rights, and the rule of law. Trump's controversial statements, provocative tweets, and confrontational style of diplomacy generated widespread controversy and criticism, both domestically and internationally.

Trump's rhetoric, particularly his use of inflammatory language and derogatory terms to describe Muslims, immigrants, and other marginalized groups, fueled anti-American sentiment and contributed to perceptions of the United States as intolerant and xenophobic. Trump's travel bans and immigration policies, which targeted predominantly Muslim-majority countries, were widely condemned as discriminatory and Islamophobic, undermining America's reputation as a beacon of freedom and opportunity.

Moreover, Trump's attacks on the media, judiciary, and other democratic institutions raised concerns about the erosion of democratic norms and values in the United States, undermining America's credibility as a champion of democracy and human rights. Trump's refusal to condemn white supremacist violence and his equivocation in the face of far-right extremism further fueled perceptions of U.S. hypocrisy and double standards in the fight against terrorism.

Furthermore, Trump's "America First" foreign policy doctrine, which prioritized narrow security interests and transactional diplomacy, raised concerns about U.S. commitment to international cooperation, alliances, and collective security efforts. Trump's criticism of NATO, the European Union, and other multilateral institutions undermined confidence in U.S. leadership and solidarity with traditional allies and partners, weakening the effectiveness of global counterterrorism efforts and eroding trust and cooperation in the fight against terrorism.

In conclusion, the Trump administration's approach to counterterrorism was characterized by a blend of continuity and divergence from previous administrations' strategies, reflecting Trump's "America First" foreign policy doctrine and emphasis on unilateralism and transactional diplomacy. While Trump's administration built upon the foundations laid by its predecessors in certain key areas, such as military force and intelligence cooperation, it also diverged from previous administrations' strategies in significant ways, including its emphasis on unilateralism, transactional diplomacy, and the prioritization of short-term security objectives over long-term stability and human rights concerns. Moreover, Trump's rhetoric and actions had a significant impact on global perceptions of the United States, shaping attitudes towards U.S. leadership, credibility, and commitment to values such as democracy, human rights, and the rule of law. As we shall explore in subsequent chapters, the legacy of the Trump administration's approach to counterterrorism continues to shape America's role in the world and its response to global challenges in the 21st century.

Chapter 14: Challenges and Future Directions

Review of Ongoing Challenges in Combating Terrorism:

Despite significant progress in the fight against terrorism over the past two decades, the threat of terrorism remains persistent and evolving, presenting ongoing challenges to national security, international stability, and global cooperation. As the global landscape continues to change and new threats emerge, policymakers and counterterrorism experts must remain vigilant and adapt their strategies to address the evolving nature of terrorism.

One of the ongoing challenges in combating terrorism is the resilience and adaptability of terrorist organizations and extremist groups, which continue to evolve their tactics, techniques, and strategies in response to counterterrorism efforts. Terrorist groups like ISIS and Al-Qaeda have demonstrated a remarkable ability to adapt to changing circumstances, exploit vulnerabilities, and exploit new technologies and platforms to advance their agendas and evade detection.

Moreover, the proliferation of non-state actors, including terrorist groups, insurgent movements, and criminal organizations, poses a significant challenge to international security and stability, as these groups operate in ungoverned spaces, exploit weak or failed states, and undermine efforts to promote peace, development, and democracy. The nexus between terrorism, organized crime, and illicit activities, such as drug trafficking, human trafficking, and arms smuggling, further complicates efforts to address the root causes of terrorism and disrupt terrorist networks.

Additionally, the rise of lone wolf terrorism and small-scale attacks carried out by individuals or small groups with limited resources and training presents a significant challenge to law enforcement and intelligence agencies, as these attackers often operate under the radar and are difficult to detect and prevent. The use of everyday objects as weapons, such as vehicles, knives, and homemade explosives, makes it challenging to anticipate and mitigate the threat posed by lone actors inspired by extremist ideologies.

Furthermore, the exploitation of cyberspace by terrorist groups and extremist organizations for propaganda, recruitment, and operational planning purposes poses a growing challenge to efforts to combat terrorism and counter violent extremism. The use of social media platforms, encrypted messaging apps, and online forums enables terrorist groups to reach a global audience, radicalize vulnerable individuals, and mobilize supporters with unprecedented speed and efficiency.

Exploration of Potential Future Threats and Trends in Terrorism:

Looking ahead, several potential future threats and trends in terrorism are likely to shape the global security landscape and challenge efforts to combat terrorism and violent extremism. These include:

1. Emerging technologies: Advances in technology, including artificial intelligence, drones, and biotechnology, are likely to be exploited by terrorist groups and extremist organizations to develop new tactics, weapons, and capabilities. The use of drones for surveillance, reconnaissance, and aerial attacks, as demonstrated by ISIS and other groups, poses a particular concern for security authorities.

2. Weaponization of emerging threats: Terrorist groups may seek to exploit emerging threats, such as pandemics, climate change, and cyber vulnerabilities, to advance their agendas and inflict harm on civilian populations. The potential for bioterrorism, cyber attacks on critical infrastructure, and disruptions to supply chains poses significant challenges for national security and public safety.

3. Transnational networks and partnerships: The globalization of terrorism and the interconnected nature of modern societies enable terrorist groups to collaborate with like-minded actors, share resources and expertise, and coordinate attacks across borders. The convergence of extremist ideologies, organized crime, and geopolitical rivalries further complicates efforts to combat terrorism and disrupt terrorist networks.

4. Radicalization and recruitment: The proliferation of extremist ideologies and the spread of disinformation and propaganda online continue to fuel radicalization and recruitment efforts by terrorist groups and extremist organizations. The use of social media algorithms, echo chambers, and online echo chambers amplify extremist narratives and polarize communities, making it

challenging to counter radicalization and prevent individuals from being drawn into violent extremism.

5. Political instability and conflict: Political instability, governance failures, and protracted conflicts in regions such as the Middle East, Africa, and South Asia provide fertile ground for the emergence and spread of terrorist groups and extremist movements. The persistence of unresolved conflicts, such as the Syrian civil war, the Israeli-Palestinian conflict, and the conflict in Afghanistan, creates conditions conducive to the proliferation of violence, extremism, and terrorism.

Recommendations for Refining Counterterrorism Strategies and Enhancing International Cooperation:

To address the ongoing challenges and future threats posed by terrorism, policymakers and counterterrorism experts must refine counterterrorism strategies and enhance international cooperation in several key areas:

1. Multilateral cooperation: Strengthening multilateral cooperation and coordination among governments, international organizations, and civil society actors is essential for effectively addressing the transnational nature of terrorism and violent extremism. This includes sharing intelligence and information, coordinating law enforcement efforts, and promoting dialogue and cooperation on counterterrorism initiatives.

2. Prevention and intervention: Investing in prevention and intervention programs aimed at addressing the root causes of terrorism, such as poverty, marginalization, political disenfranchisement, and social exclusion, is crucial for reducing the appeal of extremist ideologies and preventing radicalization and recruitment. This includes promoting inclusive governance, economic development, education, and social cohesion, as well as supporting community-led initiatives and grassroots efforts to counter violent extremism.

3. Disrupting terrorist networks: Enhancing efforts to disrupt terrorist networks, dismantle support networks, and disrupt the financing and logistics of terrorist organizations is essential for degrading their operational capabilities and preventing attacks. This includes targeting key leaders and operatives, disrupting communication channels, and disrupting the flow of resources and funding to terrorist groups.

4. Building resilience and resilience: Strengthening resilience and resilience to terrorism and violent extremism requires investing in the capacity of governments, communities, and individuals to withstand and recover from terrorist attacks and other security threats. This includes enhancing emergency preparedness and response capabilities, improving information sharing and communication channels, and promoting community resilience and cohesion.

5. Countering extremist narratives: Developing effective counter-narratives and messaging campaigns to challenge extremist ideologies, refute false narratives, and promote alternative narratives based on tolerance, inclusion, and respect for diversity is crucial for countering radicalization and preventing individuals from being drawn into violent extremism. This includes engaging with vulnerable populations, amplifying voices of moderation and moderation, and leveraging social media platforms and other communication channels to disseminate positive messages and promote constructive dialogue.

In conclusion, addressing the ongoing challenges and future threats posed by terrorism requires a comprehensive and coordinated approach that prioritizes prevention, intervention, disruption, and resilience-building efforts. By refining counterterrorism strategies, enhancing international cooperation, and promoting dialogue and collaboration among governments, civil society actors, and other stakeholders, the global community can work together to counter the evolving threat of terrorism and build a safer, more secure world for future generations.

Chapter 15: Lessons Learned and Reflections

As we reflect on America's response to global terrorism over the past two decades, it is essential to distill key lessons learned, evaluate the effectiveness of various counterterrorism measures, and consider the implications for the future of national security policy and global stability. The fight against terrorism has been marked by successes and setbacks, challenges and opportunities, and a continuous process of adaptation and learning. By examining the experiences of the past and reflecting on the lessons learned, policymakers and practitioners can refine their approaches, strengthen their capabilities, and better prepare for the evolving threats of the future.

Summarization of Key Lessons from America's Response to Global Terrorism:

1. Adaptability and Flexibility: One of the key lessons learned from America's response to global terrorism is the importance of adaptability and flexibility in the face of evolving threats. Terrorist organizations and extremist groups are constantly evolving their tactics, techniques, and strategies, requiring policymakers and practitioners to remain agile and responsive to changing circumstances. The ability to anticipate emerging threats, adjust strategies accordingly, and leverage technological advancements and innovative approaches is crucial for staying ahead of the curve in the fight against terrorism.

2. Multifaceted Approach: Another key lesson learned is the importance of adopting a multifaceted approach to counterterrorism that combines military, law enforcement, intelligence, diplomatic, and socio-economic measures. Effective counterterrorism requires a comprehensive and integrated strategy that addresses the root causes of terrorism, disrupts terrorist networks, prevents radicalization and recruitment, and builds resilience and resilience to terrorist attacks. By leveraging a range of tools and capabilities across multiple domains, policymakers can maximize their effectiveness and minimize unintended consequences.

3. Collaboration and Cooperation: Collaboration and cooperation among governments, international organizations, civil society actors, and other

stakeholders are essential for success in the fight against terrorism. No single country or entity can address the complex and transnational nature of terrorism alone. By working together, sharing information and intelligence, coordinating efforts, and pooling resources, stakeholders can enhance their collective ability to prevent terrorist attacks, disrupt terrorist networks, and address the underlying drivers of extremism and violence.

4. Protection of Civil Liberties and Human Rights: Upholding civil liberties, human rights, and the rule of law is essential for maintaining public trust and legitimacy in counterterrorism efforts. While it is necessary to take robust measures to protect national security and prevent terrorist attacks, it is equally important to respect fundamental rights and freedoms, including the rights to privacy, due process, and freedom of expression. Safeguarding civil liberties and human rights not only enhances the legitimacy of counterterrorism policies but also deprives terrorist groups of recruitment opportunities and propaganda ammunition.

5. Resilience and Adaptation: Building resilience and adaptation to terrorism requires investing in the capacity of governments, communities, and individuals to withstand and recover from terrorist attacks and other security threats. This includes enhancing emergency preparedness and response capabilities, improving information sharing and communication channels, promoting community resilience and cohesion, and fostering a culture of vigilance and resilience. By building resilience and adaptation, societies can mitigate the impact of terrorist attacks and reduce the effectiveness of terrorist propaganda and fear-mongering.

Reflections on the Effectiveness of Various Counterterrorism Measures:

In evaluating the effectiveness of various counterterrorism measures, it is essential to recognize both successes and shortcomings, strengths and weaknesses, and unintended consequences and trade-offs. While many counterterrorism measures have proven effective in preventing terrorist attacks, disrupting terrorist networks, and degrading the operational capabilities of terrorist organizations, others have raised concerns about civil liberties, human rights, and the rule of law.

1. Military Action: Military action, including airstrikes, special operations raids, and support for local partners, has played a crucial role in degrading and defeating terrorist organizations, such as ISIS and Al-Qaeda. However, the use of military force must be carefully calibrated to minimize civilian casualties, prevent the spread of extremism, and avoid exacerbating existing conflicts and instability. Additionally, military action alone is insufficient to address the underlying drivers of terrorism and may fuel resentment and radicalization in affected communities.

2. Intelligence and Law Enforcement: Intelligence and law enforcement efforts have been instrumental in disrupting terrorist plots, dismantling terrorist networks, and apprehending individuals involved in terrorist activities. Intelligence sharing, surveillance, and monitoring of communications have enabled authorities to identify and neutralize threats before they materialize. However, concerns have been raised about the scope and legality of surveillance programs, as well as the potential for abuses of power and violations of privacy rights.

3. Diplomacy and International Cooperation: Diplomacy and international cooperation are essential for addressing the root causes of terrorism, resolving conflicts, and promoting peace and stability in regions affected by terrorism. Diplomatic engagement, dialogue, and cooperation with allies and partners have facilitated intelligence sharing, coordinated military action, and promoted international norms and standards against terrorism. However, diplomatic efforts must be backed by concrete actions and commitments to be effective in addressing the underlying grievances and grievances that fuel terrorism.

4. Prevention and Counter-Radicalization: Prevention and counter-radicalization programs aimed at addressing the root causes of terrorism, countering extremist ideologies, and promoting social inclusion and resilience have shown promise in reducing the appeal of terrorism and preventing individuals from being drawn into violent extremism. By engaging with vulnerable populations, providing alternatives to extremist narratives, and building community resilience, prevention and counter-radicalization efforts can undermine the recruitment and radicalization efforts of terrorist groups. However, these programs must be carefully designed, implemented, and evaluated to ensure they are effective, evidence-based, and respectful of human rights.

5. Protection of Civil Liberties and Human Rights: Protecting civil liberties, human rights, and the rule of law is essential for maintaining public trust and legitimacy in counterterrorism efforts. Measures that violate fundamental rights and freedoms, such as mass surveillance, arbitrary detention, and torture, not only undermine the rule of law but also provide propaganda ammunition to terrorist groups and fuel resentment and radicalization in affected communities. Balancing security imperatives with respect for civil liberties and human rights is crucial for preserving the integrity and effectiveness of counterterrorism policies.

Implications for the Future of National Security Policy and Global Stability:

Looking ahead, several key implications emerge from the lessons learned and reflections on America's response to global terrorism:

1. Adaptability and Resilience: The future of national security policy and global stability will require adaptability, resilience, and agility in responding to evolving threats and challenges. Policymakers and practitioners must be prepared to anticipate emerging threats, adjust strategies accordingly, and leverage technology and innovation to stay ahead of the curve.

2. Collaboration and Cooperation: Collaboration and cooperation among governments, international organizations, civil society actors, and other stakeholders will remain essential for success in the fight against terrorism. No single country or entity can address the complex and transnational nature of terrorism alone. By working together, sharing information and intelligence, and coordinating efforts, stakeholders can enhance their collective ability to prevent terrorist attacks and disrupt terrorist networks.

3. Protection of Civil Liberties and Human Rights: Upholding civil liberties, human rights, and the rule of law will continue to be paramount in maintaining public trust and legitimacy in counterterrorism efforts. Measures that violate fundamental rights and freedoms not only undermine the rule of law but also provide propaganda ammunition to terrorist groups and fuel resentment and radicalization in affected communities.

4. Prevention and Resilience-Building: Investing in prevention and resilience-building efforts aimed at addressing the root causes of terrorism, countering extremist ideologies, and promoting social inclusion and resilience

will be critical for reducing the appeal of terrorism and preventing individuals from being drawn into violent extremism. By addressing the underlying grievances and grievances that fuel terrorism, societies can build resilience and reduce the susceptibility of vulnerable populations to radicalization and recruitment.

5. International Cooperation and Diplomacy: Diplomacy and international cooperation will remain essential for addressing the root causes of terrorism, resolving conflicts, and promoting peace and stability in regions affected by terrorism. Diplomatic engagement, dialogue, and cooperation with allies and partners will be crucial for facilitating intelligence sharing, coordinating military action, and promoting international norms and standards against terrorism.

In conclusion, America's response to global terrorism has yielded valuable lessons and insights that can inform future efforts to address the evolving threats and challenges of the 21st century. By adapting strategies, enhancing collaboration, protecting civil liberties, investing in prevention, and promoting international cooperation and diplomacy, stakeholders can work together to build a safer, more secure world for future generations.

Don't miss out!

Visit the website below and you can sign up to receive emails whenever Michael Johnson publishes a new book. There's no charge and no obligation.

https://books2read.com/r/B-A-OREFB-MMVAD

About the Author

Michael Johnson is a distinguished historian specializing in American history. With a degree in History from Harvard University, Johnson's work delves into pivotal moments, figures, and themes shaping the United States. He has authored numerous acclaimed books, offering insightful perspectives and engaging narratives. Johnson's commitment to meticulous scholarship and compelling storytelling has earned him widespread acclaim in the field. Passionate about sharing his expertise, he frequently engages in lectures and public events to foster a deeper appreciation for America's past.